Storms and blue sky

The ebb and flow in the *aberoedd* (estuaries) of the Dwyryd and Mawddach rivers in Meirionnydd brings a change to the scenery with every passing hour. Over the centuries, raging storms have shifted the sandbanks along the entire length of this coastline. The sea, and those whose livelihood has followed its course, have had a profound influence on the character of the *ardal* (vicinity) of Ardudwy – the old name for the *cantref* (hundred) which includes both Harlech and Bermo *(Barmouth)*.

Some of the early legends of the Mabinogi and Cantre'r Gwaelod are integral to Ardudwy's history. They describe how the land was swallowed by the waves and how a fleet of ships from Ireland were welcomed by the *brenin* (king) Brân at Harlech.

As well as the wealth of history and culture, nature in all its glory is also to be seen at its very best in Ardudwy. From its blue-green lakes in the high *cymoedd* (pl. of *cwm* – mountain valley) to panoramic sunsets over the western waves – the tremendous variety on display throughout every season of the year is hard to beat.

Ancient Stones

Bwlch Tyddiad – the 'Roman steps'

Carneddi Hengw

Stones are an essential element of Ardudwy and parts of the landscape are reminiscent of Conamara and western Ireland. The fields are separated by sturdy high stone walls, the result of hard labour at the time of the land enclosures some two or three centuries ago.

In Bwlch Tyddiad the so-called 'Roman Steps' follow a prehistoric path climbing from Cwm Bychan in Ardudwy through a gap in Y Rhinogydd towards the east. At some point – possibly during the era of the packhorse in the Middle Ages – stone steps were placed along the path, to make it easier for horses to cross from Harlech to the Trawsfynydd valley. There are very few Roman remains in Ardudwy – overland routes were fundamental to their empire and the Romans would have considered the *bro* (locality) to the west of the Rhinogydd as being inaccessible.

The Bwlch Tyddiad steps are only one of a number of ancient tracks which lead from the coast through the hills – evidence of how succesive waves of migrants and visitors have made landfall on this coast from the New Stone Age onwards.

There are six *cromlechi* (dolmens) dating back to about 2500 BC within a five mile radius of Harlech. These are *cromlechi porth* (portal dolmens) and the two most notable examples are to

be found behind the school in Dyffryn Ardudwy. The two now stand separately but the remains of the large *tomen* (earth mound) nearby suggest that they were originally part of a single memorial. The *cromlechi* consist of two huge stones facing each other, forming a gateway surmounted by a slanting capstone. As is usual with such designs, the gateway was closed symbolically with a slightly smaller stone.

The capstones are smooth and flat underneath and rough and convex on the upper side, suggesting that the underside was visible to those entering the burial chamber but that the upper surface was covered by a mound of stones and earth.

Only fragments of the *cromlechi* remain – traces of an ancient culture about which we now know very little. The stone in Llanbedr church is inscribed with a remarkable spiral pattern which is also to be found in Ireland and Malta and at several other ancient sites.

Dyffryn Ardudwy

Llanbedr

The Celtic Church and the Meirionnydd coast

The ancient church of Bermo, known as Llanaber, is situated to the north of the present-day town on the high ground above the spot where the Afon Mawddach (*afon* = river) formerly flowed into the sea. The church was originally consecrated to one of the old Welsh *seintiau* (saints – pl. of *sant*), Bodfan, who was a missionary in Ardudwy in the golden age of the Celtic Church. Christianity came to Wales during the Roman period when the Welsh *seintiau* established *llannau* (churches) and made contact with their fellow Celts in Éire (*Ireland*), Kernow (*Cornwall*) and Breizh (*Brittany*) a century before Saint Augustine arrived in England to spread the gospel among the pagans there.

The architecture of the ancient church at Llanaber today dates from the thirteenth century and it is now consecrated to the Virgin Mary. In the church, the two memorial stones dating from the 5th to the 7th centuries commemorate the early Christians who moved here from Breizh (*Brittany*). The church faces Bae Ceredigion and the westerly island of Enlli, that lies just off Pen Llŷn - the bodies of the *seintiau* would be carried by boat to be buried on the island during this early period.

There are three other churches in Bermo – the Catholic Church, which is consecrated to Tudwal, another of the *seintiau* of these shores; the beautiful church of John the Evangelist, dating from 1889, and the church of Dewi Sant near the harbour. This simple church was built in 1830 on the site of an old shipbuilding yard; it was used mainly by sailors to pray for safety on the sea and to give thanks for a safe passage after coming home. The 'mariners'

Eglwys Dewi Sa

church' is a familiar institution in several Celtic ports – they are also to be seen in Breizh and Kernow.

Another church with an obvious maritime connection is Llandanwg, in the sand-dunes below Llanfair near Harlech. Tanwg was a member of Cadfan Sant's retinue, who came to this coast from Breizh. Cadfan established his mother church at Tywyn and the rest of his retinue went to other parts of Meirionnydd – Tanwg came to Llandanwg; Enddwyn to Llanenddwyn, near Dyffryn Ardudwy; Dwywe to Llanddwywe near Tal-y-bont and Tegwyn to Llandecwyn a few miles north-east of Harlech.

In a terrible storm in the nineteenth century, the sea smashed the wall of Llandanwg cemetery and the gravestones were buried under great mounds of sand. Most of the gravestones were saved and the church was cleared of sand after that, but it stands today enclosed by the sand-dunes. One of the graves under the eastern window of the church is inscribed with the letters 'I.Ph'. This is believed to be the grave of Siôn Phylip of Mochras, a renowned 16th century poet from Ardudwy.

Llanenddwyn is the only cruciform church in Ardudwy and in Llanddwywe, the date of the church's construction, 1593, is to be found on the southern entrance. The Corsygedol family chapel stands on the northern side with a large screen between it and the nave of the church.

Llanenddwyn and Llanddwywe

Aber Mawddach

Despite its comparatively short length Afon Mawddach is endowed with a fine estuary. It springs from the wild moors between Trawsfynydd and Y Bala and carries with it the metallic hues of the rocks as it flows down the dramatic *dyffryn* (river valley). It follows the mountains to the sea and the wooded slopes, rocky peaks and the expansive sandbanks of the estuary combine to create a remarkably attractive vista.

At one time, the river flowed to the sea over the low lying ground where today are situated Bermo's Stryd Fawr (*high street*) and dwellings. In the Middle Ages, a small settlement was established on the slopes of the northern spit of the estuary – Llanaber – the site of the old parish church to this day. Later, cottages were built on the cliff face at Bermo – this is the oldest part of the town and it is built on a series of rock terraces, the threshold of one house being located behind the chimney pot of the one in front of it, and an intriguing network of steep paths winds between them. It is worth going for a stroll along these paths to see the craftsmanship of the old stonemasons juxtaposed with the colourful flowers of the rocky gardens.

Over the centuries, the sand-banks have spread across the estuary blocking the original entrance. By now a ridge of sand connects the reed-covered, shingle of Ynys y Brawd (the friar's island) at the mouth of the harbour to the mainland and Afon Mawddach has carved a new channel for

itself to the sea.

When Gerallt Gymro and Bishop Baldwin came on their famous journey through Wales in search of volunteers to fight in the third Crusade in 1188, they were rowed across the Mawddach estuary – there must have been a ferry service there since time immemorial for travellers between Gwynedd and the Deheubarth (southern Wales). In the 15th century there was a plan to land an army from Scotland at Bermo to support Owain Glyndŵr's rebellion.

In 1565, a report was commissioned on the ports and harbours of Meirionnydd, in response to Elizabeth I's concern that this coastline was swarming with pirates – and the queen of England certainly knew a thing or two about piracy! According to this report. there were at that time four houses and two ferries at Bermo, and herring was the staple diet of the inhabitants. By 1587 the little port had its own ship – *L'Ange de Bermo* – which imported corn mainly for the local market. There were big changes afoot, however, and with its westerly location facing the New World, Bermo would grow during the next two centuries to become one of Wales' most important ports with worldwide connections.

A Norman Castle

After centuries of sustained resistance, the military capability of the *Cymry* (the Welsh) eventually succumbed to one of the most costly invasions of the Middle Ages in 1282-3. Edward I - the king of England at the time – was one of the greediest and most merciless monarchs of his age and through a combination of a strong naval force, mercenaries from every corner of Europe and a huge fund of money, he succeeded in conquering the north-west, and in overwintering there. When Llywelyn II, the leader of the Welsh, was killed in an ambush at Cilmeri in 1282, the Welsh lost their prince and the will to fight to safeguard their identity.

It was a superficial victory for the foreign army however. It soon became obvious to Edward that he would have to prepare for the next rebellion by the Welsh. This was achieved by building a chain of huge castles around the heartland of Eryri *(Snowdonia)*. This was the costliest scheme of its kind in Europe during the Middle Ages – a manifestation of the danger which Edward still perceived as being posed by the Welsh.

Harlech was the southernmost of those castles. There had originally been a Welsh castle there but any remains thereof were destroyed by the king of England's designer, James St George of Savoy in France. St George had already won acclaim as a military architect and he followed Edward to Wales to supervise the work of erecting strong, new fortifications at Conwy, Caernarfon, Harlech and Beaumaris. They were built for warfare, and are situated close

to the sea to facilitate their supply in times of crisis, and are strategically located in a powerful position from which to challenge the hinterland.

All the Edwardian castles have a unique character and Harlech is no exception: from the outside it has a striking and powerful appearance, standing shoulder to shoulder with the peaks of Eryri, but inside it is more homely and compact. It has the same atmosphere as a large mansion, with rather a neat courtyard and fine windows in its inner walls – a castle which could also serve as a family residence.

Harlech castle was completed in 1290, in good time to withstand the great Welsh uprising of 1294-5 under the leadership of Madog ap Llywelyn. At that time, the sea and maritime support was key to the garrison's ability to hold their ground in the face of incursions by the Welsh.

In contrast to the other castles, Edward did not establish a borough in the shadow of Harlech castle to attract merchants and foreign government officials to colonise the country. No privileged town was created here to oppress the Welsh, but that did not prevent Welsh forces from attacking the castle once again during another rebellion in 1400.

9

The Home and Senedd of Owain Glyndŵr

It is ironic that the most famous person ever to make his home in Harlech castle was the Welsh national hero Owain Glyndŵr. It was obvious that he too had an eye for a favourable site.

Wales had suffered more than a century of barbaric government in the shadow of Edward I's castles and towns. A huge number of men and boys had been killed as a precaution in case of rebellion and according to English records, hundreds more women, children and old people were also slaughtered. After 1282, taxes in Wales increased by six hundred per cent – the English crown was bankrupt after the costly war. Then, the first anti-Welsh laws were passed – the Welsh could neither hold office nor possess land in a town nor trade beyond the walls of a town; they were not allowed to carry arms and unable to accuse an Englishman of committing any offence; *Cymraeg* (the Welsh language) was forbidden as a public language and a Welshman could be executed without the sanction of a court of law if he were caught in a town after nightfall.

Six hundred years ago, the Welsh had had enough of this racial oppression. Owain of Glyndyfrdwy, which lies to the south of Rhuthun, rose up as a leader and together with three hundred followers, attacked the town of Rhuthun and razed it to the ground in September 1400. Over the years that followed every English town in Wales was attacked and burnt; many of the 'castles of conquest' were attacked too, several even being successfully captured.

Glyndŵr's flag in Harlech today

One of the castles which fell into the hands of Glyndŵr's army in the spring of 1404 was Harlech. He moved his headquarters and family there, and for four years this had a very positive effect on his campaign. During that period Glyndŵr received a number of European ambassadors there and in 1405 and 1406, a Welsh *senedd* (parliament) was held there three times.

A large English army of some one thousand men, arrived to besiege Harlech castle in 1408. It was a long siege throughout the spring and summer and was met by staunch Welsh resistance. Traces of the prolonged bombardment are still to be seen on the defences, which resulted in the castle's evacuation in February 1409. Marged, Owain's wife and Catrin, his daughter and her children were taken to the Tower of London but Owain himself managed to escape.

After the promise of Glyndŵr's ascendancy, when the foundations of modern Wales were laid in both word and deed, Glyndŵr's fortunes started to ebb. He was under constant pressure from the English armies and the country became gravely impoverished as a result of the continuing state of war. After fifteen years of rebellion, Owain and his small band of faithful followers disappeared from the history books to the world of mythology. It is not known where he died, but his great dream of Wales enjoying full national status amongst the countries of Europe, lives on.

The Plastai of Ardudwy and the Flames of Independence

As Glyndŵr's story became legend, the responsibility for defending different *ardaloedd* (pl. of *ardal*) of Wales from the oppressive English penal laws fell to the *uchelwyr* (noblemen). Various families from the great *plastai* (houses/mansions) of Ardudwy – Maes-y-neuadd, Cwm Bychan, Corsygedol and others, were descendants of the old Welsh *tywysogion* (princes). They maintained the traditional role of the Welsh *uchelwr* (nobleman) – defending their land and people and providing patronage for the *beirdd* (poets) and local culture.

In the 15th century, the Welsh were looking for a national leader to succeed Glyndŵr. People started to whisper the name of Harri, one of the descendants of the Tudur family from Penmynydd, Môn, who was in exile in Breizh, but through his grandfather's marriage could claim succession to the English throne through the House of Lancaster. Sometime between 1460 and 1485, the period of the Wars of the Roses, Gruffudd Fychan, Corsygedol, built a house on the edge of the Mawddach estuary, Tŷ Gwyn (white house) at Bermo, which has been restored and its upper floor recently turned into a museum. According to tradition, Jasper Tudur, Harri Tudur's uncle, sailed here and met with the *uchelwyr* of the *ardal* at Tŷ Gwyn in order to gain support for the rebellion. There was talk that Harri would land his Breton army on the shores of the Mawddach estuary and march to Bosworth Field from there, but eventually it was the harbour at Aberdaugleddau *(Milford Haven)* which was chosen by the *Tuduriaid* (Tudors). Tŷ Gwyn was a popular sailors'

Tŷ Gwyn

Corsygedol

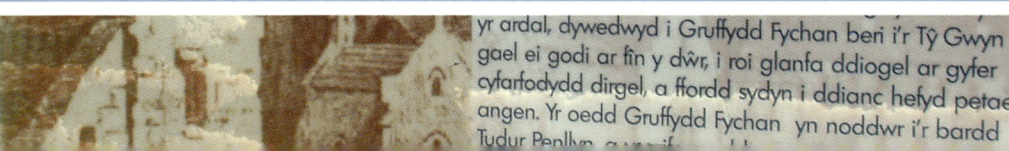

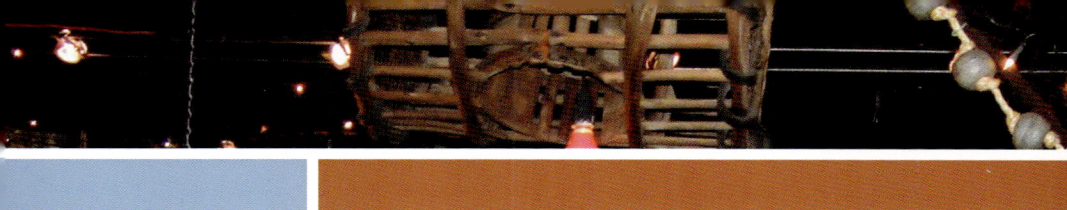

tavern throughout the golden age of the port and you can still enjoy a meal and slake your thirst downstairs, experiencing the atmosphere of the old days.

The Welsh *uchelwyr* gave their support to the victorious Harri Tudur, but having attained the throne in London, the king disregarded the needs of his fellow Welsh to a large extent. Some of the *uchelwyr* became quite Anglicised in their language and ways, going to live in London and forgetting about their people back home. Others stayed true to the dreams of the Welsh.

One of these was General Henry Lloyd, Cwm Bychan, one of the Llwyd family, who was descended from the *Tywysogion* of Powys. He saw an opportunity to strike a blow against the English crown in his support for the Jacobeans. He went to France, became involved with the Irish Brigade who supported any enemy of England and joined the Jacobean rebellion in 1745.

Ellis Wynne was one of the Wynn family from Maes-y-neuadd on his mother's side. He inherited the *plasty* (mansion) of Y Lasynys near Harlech and became the rector of Llandanwg parish in 1704. He was the author of a work of colourful prose which satirises sinners on their way to hell, and is one of the great classics of Welsh literature. Maes-y-neuadd is now a luxurious hotel and restaurant and Y Lasynys belongs to a local trust, who have restored it to its former glory and opened its doors to the public.

Y Lasynys Fawr

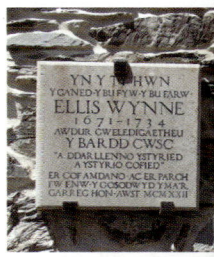

13

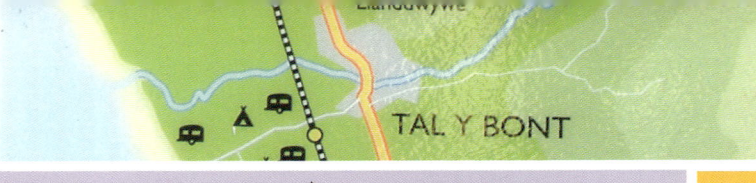

Ffyrdd y Porthmyn - The Drovers' Roads

From the end of the Middle Ages until the arrival of the railways, the Welsh *porthmyn* (drovers) would drive thousands of cattle, sheep, pigs and geese each year from the mountain pastures to the rich grasslands of south-east England to be fattened up for the markets there. This was a journey of hundreds of miles, often over rough, and remote highland terrain. Amongst the dangers were wolves, highwaymen as well as severe weather conditions. Wales had its Wild West and its heroes on the droving trails long before Hollywood romanticised the cowboys of the New World.

The slopes, mountains and river valleys of Ardudwy were ideal for rearing good stock. The *porthmyn* would be local men, since the farmers were entrusting them with responsibility for their livestock throughout the journey. Each droving expedition contained an element of financial risk and investment. Blacksmiths were paid to shoe the cattle and sheep and for putting leather shoes or tar and sand on the feet of the geese before driving them over the mountains. At their journey's end, the *porthmyn* would be at the mercy of the marketplace and were responsible for ensuring the safe delivery of money back to Ardudwy which would be needed to support the local economy for another year. It is hardly surprising that the *porthmy*n were referred to as the 'Welsh Armada'. Although there are stories about an occasional deceitful *porthmon* (sing. of *porthmyn*) absconding with the takings from the market, generally speaking *porthmyn* were highly respected individuals.

No one had a right to a droving licence unless they were over 30 years old, married and a house owner. The *porthmon* himself would travel on horseback – but it was a different story for the other cattle hands – the rather tough and violent men and young lads who would be in charge of the herd or flock. These had a bad reputation for being rather too fond of their beer, feats of strength, fighting, wrestling and womanising as they moved from place to place on their journey. It is said that English publicans used to remove the curtains from the windows and take up the carpets when they heard that the Welsh *porthmyn* were on their way!

The droving centres in Ardudwy were Llanfair, Llanbedr and Tal-y-bont – there are gravestones in the sandy churchyard of Llandanwg for the Roberts family, famous *porthmyn* from that *bro* (locality). Other notable drovers were the Puws of Llanfair. Several place names record the drovers' trail through the mountain passes – the steep climb through Bwlch y Rhiwgyr (herd's hill pass), and Llety Lloegr (England's rest) – the last refuge for the *porthmyn* before crossing the mountains for England), where the herds used to be shoed. The remains of their tracks can be seen winding up the slopes and ruins of the old drovers' taverns are to be found here and there on the mountainsides and an occasional wild pine by the side of the cart-tracks marking their route across the bare terrain.

Sgethin inn

Pont Fadog and Llety Lloegr

15

The Port of Bermo

One of the main reasons for the prosperity of the port of Bermo was the development of the wool industry. This was the most important industry in Meirionnydd, with weavers making cloth in their cottages and an increasing number of woollen mills being built. Until 1770, most of the produce from the rural valleys would go to the weekly market at Shrewsbury. The English monopoly was broken and in 1772, a depot was established in Bermo for the long, white cloth known as *gweoedd* (webs), from where it was exported to several parts of the world – including Europe, North America and Mexico.

Meirionnydd's woollen mills produced rough flannels from the fleece of mountain sheep and after mixing it with the fleece of sheep from abroad, this was mainly sold as clothing for slaves in North and South America and the Caribbean. Ships would sail regularly from Bermo across the Atlantic to the ports of Charleston and New Orleans, both centres of slavery.

Oak from the slopes of the Mawddach valley was especially suitable for shipbuilding which grew to be an important industry on the banks of the river. Between 1750 and 1865, a total of 318 ships were built along the Mawddach estuary, as far up as Llanelltyd – many of them of a considerable size. With the development of the slate industry in Eryri, there was an increasing demand for even more ships. The golden age lasted until the 1860s when the railway reached the town.

The port of Bermo was dredged in 1797

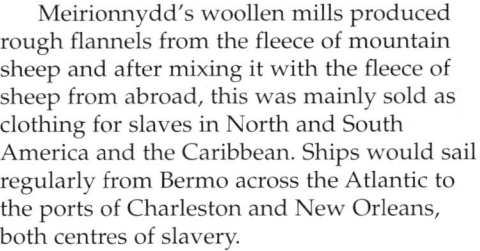

16

and 200 local merchants invested in undertaking to make the harbour safer and more accessible. Nowadays, only a handful of fishing boats and pleasure craft are left to lay claim to the old connection with the sea.

Several of the buildings in the vicinity of the old harbour have their own story. Among them is the Seamen's Mission – a zinc hut which was erected next to the railway bridge in 1890 to offer shelter and comfort to sailors who called in on their journey. This is the only one of its kind to have survived in Wales and it was restored in 1984. It is open to the public, and it contains an exhibition of old pictures and newspaper cuttings and a billiards room.

Also by the harbour is the Hen Dŷ Crwn (old roundhouse). Its stone walls are two feet thick and the chimney which rises from the middle of the steep-slanting slate roof is purely ornamental. It was decided to erect the roundhouse in 1834 because respectable people of the town were concerned about the behaviour of an increasing number of drunken sailors in the port. Inside the Tŷ Crwn there are two cells, one for men and the other for women, and an outer door to each. Drunks would be kept there overnight until they had sobered up sufficiently to appear before the magistrates' bench. When the police station was opened in the town in 1861, the building was no longer needed but it has been restored, and it now receives the attention it deserves as part of the harbour's heritage.

Shipwrecks and rescues at sea

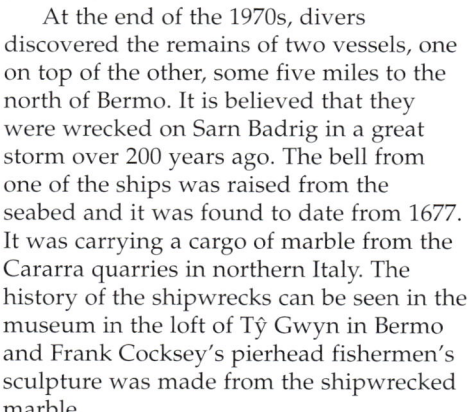

Under the sea to the west of Harlech and Bermo lie lowlands which were submerged at the end of the Ice Age. A folk memory has been preserved concerning this event in the old legend of Cantre'r Gwaelod (the lowland hundred) and the remains of tree-roots which appear at low tide give credence to the story. Also at low tide Sarn Badrig (Patricks' causeway) can be seen. This is an extended rocky ridge under the sea stretching for miles towards the south-west of Ynys Fochras. This, according to the legend, was one of the dykes of Cantre'r Gwaelod. The causeway was a nightmare for sailors and several ships have foundered on it over the centuries.

At the end of the 1970s, divers discovered the remains of two vessels, one on top of the other, some five miles to the north of Bermo. It is believed that they were wrecked on Sarn Badrig in a great storm over 200 years ago. The bell from one of the ships was raised from the seabed and it was found to date from 1677. It was carrying a cargo of marble from the Cararra quarries in northern Italy. The history of the shipwrecks can be seen in the museum in the loft of Tŷ Gwyn in Bermo and Frank Cocksey's pierhead fishermen's sculpture was made from the shipwrecked marble.

Before the Lifeboat Institute was established in 1824, the inhabitants of Bermo already provided their own life-saving service at sea. A boat was kept in the cellar of Pen y cei (end of the quay), the

18 *Sarn Badrig*

building in which the Maritime Museum and the harbourmaster's office are now situated. Previously, the brave crews would have nothing except oars and sails to assist them in saving sailors from the jaws of the storms. The RNLI station was opened in Bermo in 1828 but motorboats were not used by the service until 1904. Rowing boats ceased to be used in 1948.

Fast, inshore rescue craft came into operation in the Lifeboat station in Bermo in 1967. By then, the demands on the service were changing in line with the changing nature of maritime traffic. Now, instead of ocean going ships running into trouble in storms, it was visitors in small boats and inexperienced swimmers who were responsible for most of the emergency callouts. Having a high-speed craft which was easily launched near the beach was essential. This boat is located near the old bathhouse and it can be on its way with a crew of three within a few seconds. It can forge its way through a heavy swell and reach places which would be impossible for a larger lifeboat. Over the years the lifeboat has rescued dozens of individuals in distress and up to the year 2000, the total number of people saved by the lifeboat at Bermo was 522, and a number of crew members have received medals in recognition of their exceptional courage in carrying out their voluntary work at sea.

19

Llanfair Slates

There is plenty of high quality Cambrian slate under the Rhinogydd in north-west Meirionnydd, but the rock in this *ardal* is inaccessible and difficult to work. The only place where it could be reached easily was at Llanfair near Harlech which, for a while, became the site of a major quarrying community. Before the days of the railway, Llanfair slates were transported to Pensarn and exported on ships from there.

Llanfair was a quarry which used the underground method of accessing the slate – huge cathedral-like caverns were opened up in the heart of the mountain from the 1860s onwards. A series of layers of good quality slate were worked which descended in five galleries below the surface. This was the only quarry in the *ardal* and the history of its production was stormy; it is possible that it was the cost of its method of operation which was responsible for this. The quarry was closed after a few years but re-opened at the beginning of the twentieth century. The First World War put an end to its activity for a while, then it became a site for crushing rocks for a powder which was used in the production of tiles, employing twenty men. Explosives were stored in the safety of the caverns during the Second World War.

There are still a few quayside buildings to be seen at Pensarn, the relics of the export trade which was conducted from there at one time. After the Cambrian

Railway reached the *ardal,* slates were transported by train.

The caverns were opened as a visitor attraction in the 1960s. With the aid of electricity and powerful lighting, it is possible for visitors today to see the wonder of these underground caves which were never seen by the quarrymen themselves who were hewing the rock by candlelight over a hundred years ago. It was in these caverns that some of the scenes from *First Knight* were filmed. A few of the original buildings still remain and many of the adits have been made safe and are open to the public, where old tools and wagons are on display. There is also a café and a shop selling slate crafts.

The crags of the Rhinogydd are renowned for their mineral wealth – to the south-east, between the peaks and the town of Dolgellau, lie the most important gold mines on the island of Britain. Between Bermo and Bont-ddu in the south and Harlech and Trawsfynydd in the north, 44,000 tonnes of manganese were extracted from the western slopes of the Rhinogydd: there were 17 mines in all in the period between 1892-1928. Remains of buildings are still to be seen by the roadside along the Afon Artro valley – Coed and Dôl Bebin – but most of them are located in very remote places.

Salem yn y wlad (Salem in the countryside)

Upstream from the village of Llanbedr and at the edge of Cwm Nantcol, stands the chapel of Salem Cefn Cymerau, one of the most famous chapels in Wales. In 1908, the artist Curnow Vosper painted a picture in this simple little rural chapel, paying a few shillings to the congregation for their service as models. Prints of the painting were used to sell *Sunlight* soap – a free copy with every ten pounds of soap. The soap sold extremely well in Wales and to this day the Salem print is a common feature in many Welsh homes.

Salem is a chapel with two doors either side. In the picture the 'congregation' has gathered for the morning service – it is ten minutes to ten on the clock. Some of the worshippers look suitably devout with their heads bowed in their hands but the main character is a woman wearing a Welsh shawl who looks as if she is walking towards the back door. In the folds of her shawl on her left arm, according to some, the bearded face of the devil can be seen.

What is the significance of the picture? Vosper denied that his intention was to belittle the chapel and its congregation, but was it unintentional that the devil's face is in the shawl? The shawl was lent by the wife of a vicar from Harlech – it is a luxury item and it was set carefully over a statue so that the artist could show off the detail of its pattern.

The names of the characters were recorded: Siân Owen, Ty'n y Fawnog, was the old woman, a cheerful and devout individual apparently, and the story about

the devil in the shawl was very hurtful for her.

Another strange fact which adds to the mystery of the picture is that the characters are wearing clothes from the first half of the 19th century. The artist had one high crowned hat at his disposal and this was modelled by each of the women in turn. The picture is sure to remain a talking point for some time, but it is a work of art which is very close to the hearts of the Welsh. It did not do any harm to the artist either; he had studied art in Paris and painted in Breizh, but the picture of Salem was the turning point of his career, after which he enjoyed considerable fame.

The doors of the Salem Baptist chapel opened for the first time in 1850 and the custom was to baptise chapel members in the waters of the Afon Artro which flows nearby. To this day you can sense the atmosphere encapsulated in T. Rowland Hughes' poem which is still to be seen on the wall of the building:

Y cwmni gwledig ar ddiarffordd hynt…
Countryfolk coming from afar –
Siân Owen, Wiliam Siôn and Owen Siôn
and Robat Wilias erstwhile of Cae Meddyg
And sweet-voiced Laura from Ty'n y Buarth.

The Railway and Pont Bermo

By 1865, the *Aberystwyth and Welsh Coast Railway* had reached Y Friog on the southern side of the Mawddach estuary. Travellers who wished to continue their journey up the coast had to cross the estuary to Bermo by ferry, a ferry which still offers its services to this day.

According to travellers at that time, this arrangement was by no means ideal. It involved a two mile journey in a horse and carriage followed by a quarter of a mile on foot across the rough beach. The passengers would then have to cross an often choppy half mile stretch of water over the estuary. If the tide was low, the boat would land on shingle in the middle of the river, where the passengers would have to disembark and walk to a boat on the other side of the shingle to reach Bermo.

Before long, work was commenced on bridging the estuary. The bridge has 113 wooden arches and eight metal sections. Each one of the iron pillars which support the structure is eight feet across and they had to be sunk 120 feet below sea level in order to ensure that they stood on solid rock. A 'swing bridge' was designed to be part of the structure to allow tall ships to sail up the river.

The bridge was opened initially to horses and carts in June 1867; in October of the same year a steam train crossed the estuary for the first time ever. In 1900 the 'swing bridge' was replaced by a steel bridge which swivels to allow ships to pass through.

The bridge was under threat in the 1980s after it was discovered that a small maggot called *feredo navalis* had been enjoying slap-up meals in 69 of the wooden pillars. Some of the

holes were several feet wide by then. Bermo bridge was closed between October 1980 and April 1986, and for a while it looked as if the Cambrian coast line was being wound down completely. However, central government was successfully persuaded to invest in the line and £1.8 million was spent to repair the bridge. Today, Pont y Bermo is one of the longest bridges in this island spanning 2292 feet (nearly half a mile) across one of the most beautiful estuaries in Wales.

On the other side of the estuary from Bermo there is another railway line accessible on a ferry which crosses the mouth of the river. This is the narrow gauge line at Y Friog (*Fairbourne*); a mere fifteen inches wide and two and a half miles in length. In contrast to some of Wales's other narrow gauge railways, this is not in fact an industrial line. It was built to transport building material to the village of Y Friog by Arthur McDougall (the flour manufacturer) in 1895. It was kept open afterwards as an attraction for visitors to the new village. The halt between Y Friog station and the head of the peninsula has the longest name in the world:

Gorsafawddachardraigodanheddogleddol-lonpenrhynareurdraethceredigion

This made-up name is unfortunately full of grammatical inconsistencies but refers to Mawddach station at ebb tide, jagged rocks and the golden beach of Ceredigion and has obviously been devised to compete with its famous counterpart in Llanfairpwllgwyngyll in Ynys Môn.

Summer Visitors from England

The tourist industry plays a prominent part in the economy of the *ardal*. The acres of caravan parks between the sea and the mountains bear witness to the fact that careful planning was not a high priority when the industry was developing in the past. By now, sustainable tourism acknowledges the need to protect the land and the coast as well as appreciating the wealth of the indigenous history and culture which are integral to Ardudwy.

There are over two hundred years of history behind the modern industry. The first hotel, Corsygedol, was built in Bermo in 1795. Visitors had begun to flock there for sea bathing – something which was very fashionable at the time. The first bathing machines were dragged to Bermo beach in 1798, allowing women (and men!) of a shy and modest disposition to change using these static cabins and wait for the tide. They could then descend the steps concealed by curtains so that no one could see their legs! Later, more flexible machines were developed which were drawn towards the waves by horses.

Bathing was also good for your health. Many infirm visitors would come to Bermo for that reason. The common scurvygrass was popular too, the plant growing freely on the banks of the Mawddach estuary which was used by those suffering from scurvy.

A road was forged through the rocks

26

of the estuary from Bermo to Bont-ddu in 1798, facilitating overland travel to the town. Gwesty'r Llew (the lion hotel) was built and the foundations of the present-day Stryd Fawr were laid in 1829 but a big difference was seen following the building of Pont Bermo (*pont* – bridge) in 1867, bringing the railway to the town. The number of merchant ships declined – 150 ships called in the harbour in 1867; this number dropped to less than twelve by 1876. However, more and more summer visitors kept on coming to the *ardal*. Suitable accommodation was built for them, especially in Rhodfa'r Môr. A harbour wall and new promenade were built in the 1930s following a terrible storm in 1923. Another promenade was built to Ynys y Brawd in 1972, one effect of which was that the harbour filled with sediment from the river.

The beach at Bermo won the European blue flag in 1997.

The Dewi Sant golf course at Harlech is considered to be the best in north Wales.

Harlech college and the golf course on the dunes

Seeing value in heritage

Fanny Talbot – one of the most generous and influential residents of Bermo – lived in Ty'n y Ffynnon, above the old town. In March 1895, she donated Dinas Oleu, four and a half acres of upland which abutted her house, to the National Trust. This was the first property the National Trust had ever owned.

The National Trust was established by friends of Fanny Talbot with the intention of safeguarding natural beauty and buildings of historical interest for future generations. There was a close connection between them and Bermo since it was under John Ruskin's influence that the Guild of St George was established as an experimental estate on the heights above the town. John Ruskin was born in London and became a renowned art critic and social thinker in the Victorian Age. His words inspired movements such as the National Trust, the Society for the Protection of Ancient Buildings, the Labour Movement and the Arts and Crafts Movement. He promoted the arts and museums for the working class and he was keen to put his experimental ideas into practice.

In 1875, through the generosity of Fanny Talbot, he received land and 13 cottages on the slopes of the old town to facilitate his attempt to create his Utopia there. These were 'Ruskin's Cottages' and some of the basic principles behind the project were that the rents should not be raised, that the tenants were of good character and paid the lease, that they were to receive assistance if they were ill and that the cottages were improved to create more comfortable homes

for them.

One of the tenants of Ruskin's Cottages for a while was Auguste Guyard from France. He himself had attempted to establish an ideal society in his hometown of, Frotey-les-Vesoul in the heart of France. Having had some success, he ran into trouble and eventually accepted an offer from Fanny Talbot to come and live in one of the cottages; one of his daughters had already made her home in Ardudwy. He adapted to his new life quickly, undertaking to teach his neighbours how to grow vegetables and herbs in the terraced gardens of the old town. He showed them the value of medicinal plants, caring tenderly for the sick of the *ardal*. Auguste Guyard was a perfect tenant and when he died in 1883, he was buried according to his wishes 150 feet further up the mountain from Ty'n y Ffynnon, in a spot overlooking the rock and harbour of Bermo. His grave can be seen to this day and his handiwork still lives on in the gardens which were created so industriously by him on the sunny terraces of the slope.

In 1961 Ty'n y Ffynnon was destroyed by a fire. A new house has now been built, but there are memorial plaques on the gable walls to commemorate the former owner whose vision was so far-reaching and who was so generous in her contribution to society.

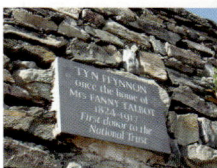

Modern-day Attractions

Mountain pastures running down to the sea, beaches stretching for miles, narrow, wooded river and high mountain valleys and lakes and peaks – there is an abudance of views and peaceful beauty spots to discover when you explore the *ardal* between Harlech and Bermo. With such a choice of footpaths, it is no wonder that there is no scarcity of walkers in these parts.

An interesting spot on the coast to experience a range of activities associated with the sea is Ynys Fochras, near Llanbedr. The road to it crosses the marsh which is submerged at high-tide and there is a charge for using the resources according to the number of people in the car. There are eating places, shops and a camp site. You can watch birds, fish, go on a boat, collect shellfish, watch seals, not to mention swimming in the sea.

Maes Artro, Llanbedr is a village offering a variety of experiences. At one time the buildings housed the crew of aircraft which flew from the nearby airfield. An occasional reminder of the war remains to this day. There is an indoor heritage museum depicting life in a rural village. There is also a sealife aquarium, as well as nature trails, an adventure park for children, craft shops and eating places.

The *ardal* is very attractive to visitors who enjoy outdoor pursuits. The ancient paths, the drovers' roads, the old, industrial railways and nature trails

create plenty of opportunities for both walkers and cyclists. One can plan circular walks and the coastal path of Meirionnydd is worth exploring. At Llanfair near Harlech children can see a presentation of the heritage of the countryside at a farm park, an all-weather attraction – including goats, rabbits, mules, pigs, ducks and hens.

Historical events are commemorated in Harlech from time to time – in 2004 there was a celebration to commemorate the period when Owain Glyndŵr lived and held a Welsh *senedd* in the castle. Bermo is also famous for its festivals. At the end of June, the Three Peaks Yacht Race is held, which combines sailing and mountain running, which starts from Bermo, visiting the peaks of Yr Wyddfa (from Caernarfon), Scafell Pike (from Whitehaven) and Ben Nevis (from Fort William). It is a non-stop race of 390 miles at sea, 75 miles on mountains and the current record is two days, nine hours. In addition to this, there are music, art, motorbike and walking festivals to be enjoyed throughout the year in the town.

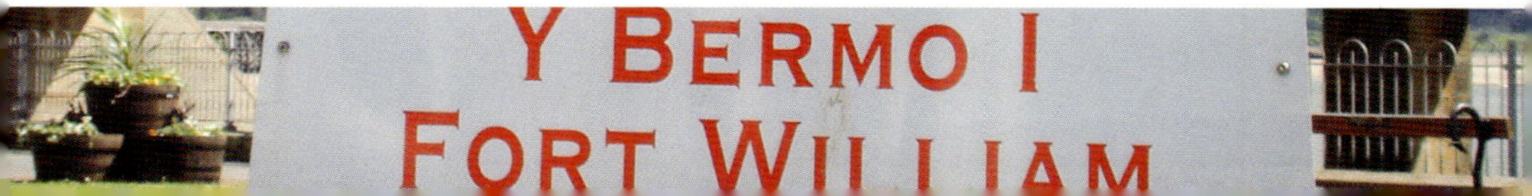